Looking *at* Pictures

Light and Dark

Joy Richardson

FRANKLIN WATTS
LONDON • SYDNEY

First published in Great Britain in 1997
This edition 1999
Franklin Watts
96 Leonard Street
London EC2A 4RH

Franklin Watts Australia
14 Mars Road
Lane Cove
NSW 2066

0 7496 3571 1

10 9 8 7 6 5 4 3

Dewey Decimal Classification Number: 758

A CIP catalogue record for this book is
available from the British Library.

Editor: Sarah Ridley
Designer: Louise Thomas
Art Director: Robert Walster

Photographs:
Reproduced by courtesy of the Trustees of the National Gallery, London ter Brugghen/The Concert cover, pgs 6-7, 26 (detail), Geertgen/The Nativity pgs 4-5, Claude/A Seaport pgs 8-9, Wright/Experiment with the Air Pump pgs 12-13, 29 (detail), Pissarro/Paris, the Boulevard Montmartre pgs 16-17, Monet/The Beach at Trouville pgs 22-23, 29 (detail); reproduced by courtesy of the Prado Museum, Madrid Fortuny/Landscape with a Human Figure pgs 20-21; © photo RMN/Vermeer/The Lacemaker pgs 10-11, 28 (detail); © Tate Gallery, London Turner/Norham Castle, Sunrise pgs 14-15, Whistler/Nocturne in Blue and Gold: Old Battersea Bridge pgs 18-19, Paula Rego/ The Dance pgs 24-25, 27 (detail).

Printed in Belgium

Contents

What happens to colours in the dark?
Where do shadows fall?
How do you paint sunshine?

Explore the pictures in this book to discover some artists' answers.

The Nativity, at Night

painted by Geertgen

The darkness of night is pierced
with light as Jesus is born in a stable.

Can you find nine pairs of eyes fixed on the baby?

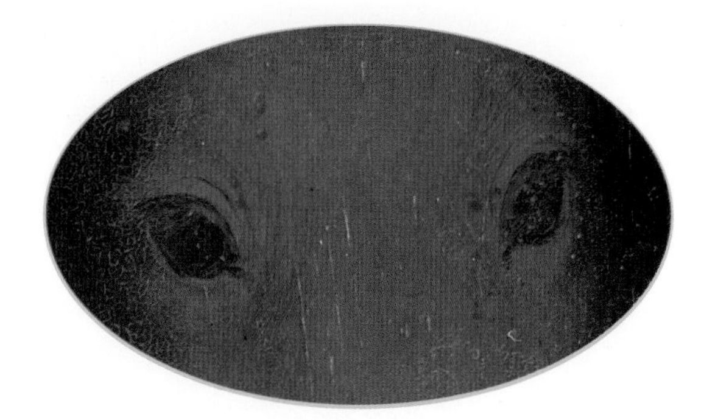

Who is watching in the shadows?

Can you see ...

a shining angel,

bonfire light

and holy light from the baby?

The Concert

painted by ter Brugghen

Flickering flames pattern the darkness
with light and shadows.

Look carefully to see where the light reaches from the lamp and the candle.

The face stands out, spot-lit in the darkness.

Shadows fall in the folds of the clothes.

Light rounds the grapes and makes them look real.

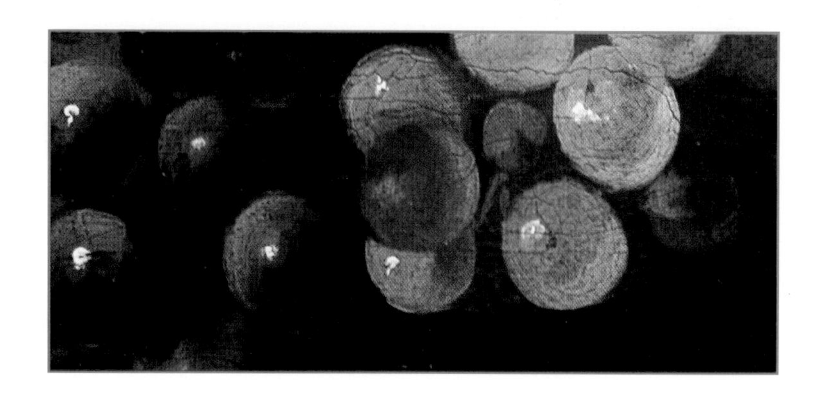

A Seaport

painted by Claude

The evening sun sinks in the sky,
casting a glow across the harbour.

The ship looks black against the sun.

Light shimmers across the water.

The low sun makes long shadows.

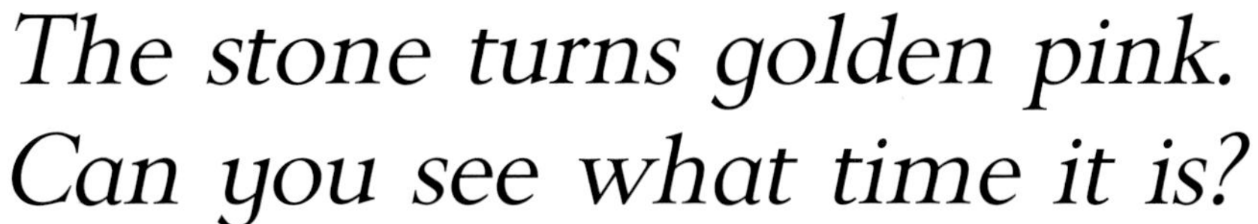

The stone turns golden pink. Can you see what time it is?

The Lacemaker

painted by Vermeer

The lacemaker needs light from a window to see what she is doing.

Light shows the shape of the work box ...

and the curves of her face.

Look how colours darken where the shadows fall.

Which direction is the light coming from?

Experiment with the Air Pump

painted by Wright

Light spotlights the people
watching this experiment with a bird.

Who is curious?
Who is thoughtful?
Who can't bear to look?

A hidden light shines through the glass to light the scene.

The moon breaks through the clouds.

Norham Castle, Sunrise

painted by Turner

The rising sun fills the air
with light on a fresh new day.

The sun's brightness fades the sky to the palest blue.

Look how the mist hangs in the valley.

Animals come to the shining water.

The hazy castle stands out like a bruise.

Paris, the Boulevard Montmartre at Night

painted by Pissarro

The artist paints a dark wet night
looking down a busy street.

People lose their colour in the dark.

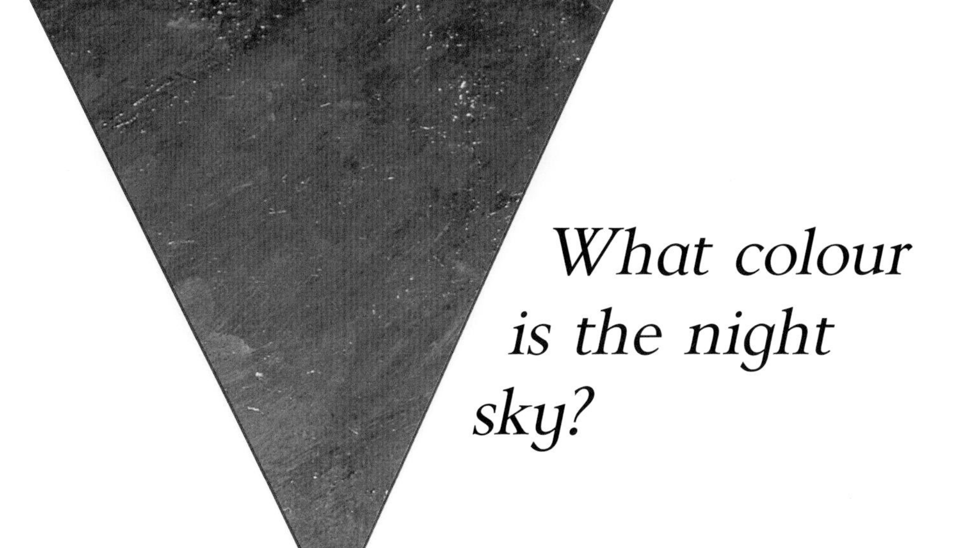

What colour is the night sky?

Shop lights,

street lights

and carriage lights brighten up the night.

The wet pavement reflects the light.

Nocturne in Blue and Gold

painted by Whistler

Night creeps over the misty river
turning everything blue.

Sparks from fireworks spatter the sky.

Buildings merge with their reflections.

Water and sky melt into each other.

Shadowy people cross the bridge.

Landscape with a Human Figure

painted by Fortuny

The garden shimmers in the light
while a dog dozes in the shade.

Strong light makes colours brighter ...

and shadows deeper.

The dog lies almost hidden in the shade.

Look how light and shade colour the pebbles on the path.

The Beach at Trouville

painted by Monet

The midday sun shines brightly
on the beach, between the clouds.

The dress glares white in the sunlight.

Look at the light on the parasol, and the dark underneath.

Light shines through the moving clouds.

The faces are shaded from the light.

The Dance

painted by Rego

People young and old
dance round by the light of the moon.

Moonlight spills across the sea ...

and edges the earth with silver.

Look at the colours in the inky blue sky.

The whirling dancers cast long shadows. Whose is this?

Lighting Effects

Lighting colours

Colours need light to show them up.

Roll a piece of card to make a tube. Look through it as you bring it down to touch your sleeve, or the table or a book cover. Watch the colours grow dim.

Focus a torch on objects around you and watch the colours brighten.

Try painting the same patch of colour to show how it looks in bright light and low light.

For help, look back at pages 8, 16 and 20.

Shadow play

Look at the shadows falling softly or sharply on the ground outside, or on the floor indoors.

Try painting a shadow, showing the surface on which it falls.

For help, look back at page 24.

Shaped by light

Light and shade on curves and corners show how things are shaped.

Place a box or drop a piece of material on a table near a window. Look carefully and paint it to show where the light and shade fall. Try adding white or a little black to make the colour lighter or darker.

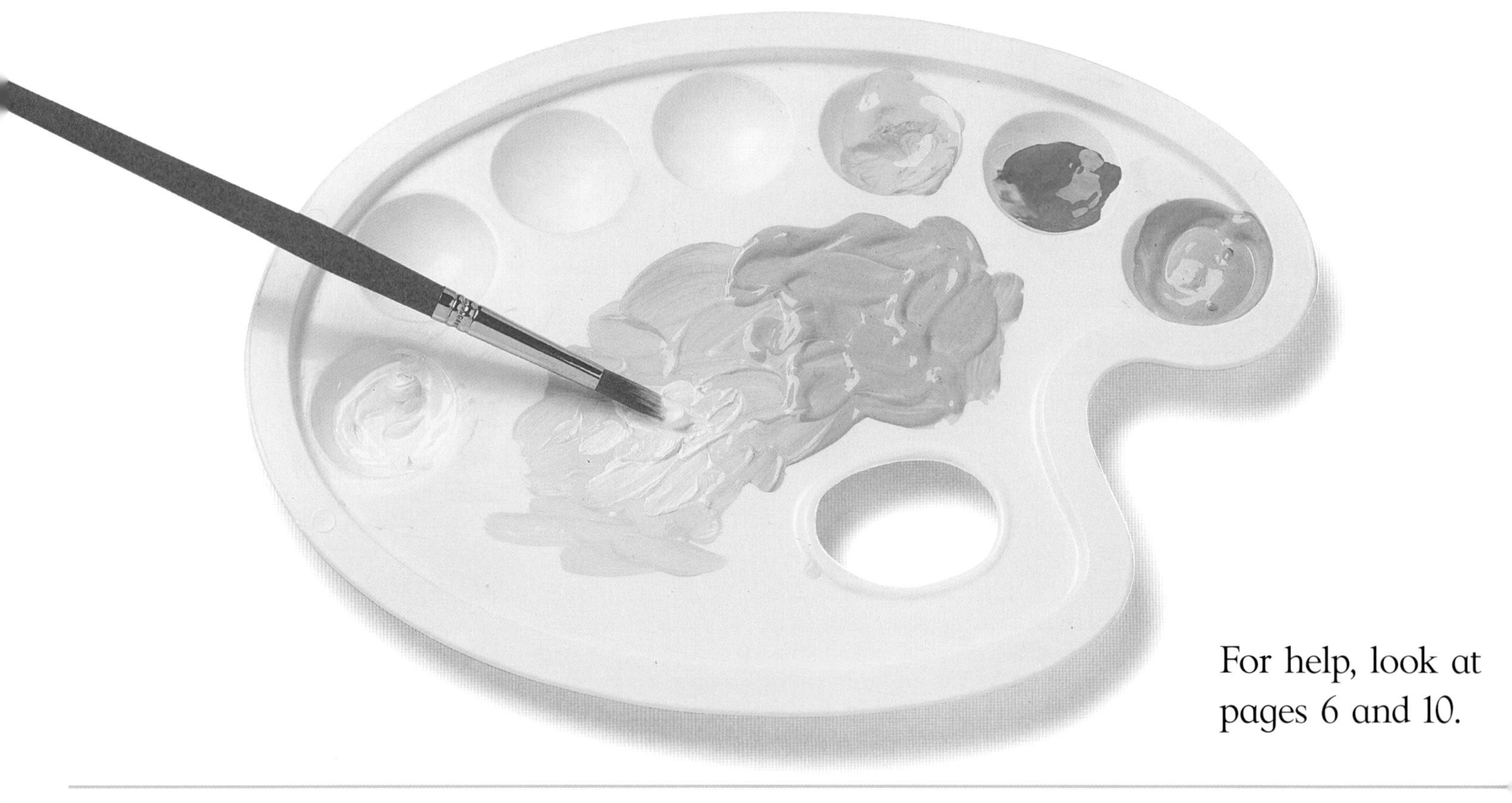

For help, look at pages 6 and 10.

Sky light

Sky colours change with the weather and the time of day.

Look closely at the sky and try painting a small patch.

For help, look at pages 14, 16 and 22.

Faces in the dark

A torch or a candle flame lights the darkness in patches and leaves deep shadows.

Darken the room as much as possible. Use a torch to light a face from one direction. Try painting the effect this makes.

For help, look back at pages 4 and 12.

More about the pictures in this book

The Nativity at Night

Geertgen tot Sint Jans (about 1455-1495) worked in Holland, making religious paintings for the monastery of the Brethren of St. John. In this picture of Jesus's birth, the main source of light is the baby. This refers to a story of the holy child shining brighter than any earthly light.

The Concert

Hendrick ter Brugghen (about 1588-1629) was Dutch. He learnt the dramatic use of lighting, with pools of light set off against deep shadows, from the Italian artist Caravaggio. Ter Brugghen also learned to use light to make details, such as the grapes, look real and natural.

A Seaport

Claude Lorrain (1600-1682) was French but went to live in Italy. Claude looked closely at nature but also used his imagination to construct beautiful views. People especially admired the way he showed light filling the atmosphere. No-one had ever painted the full effect of the sun like this before.

The Lacemaker

Jan Vermeer (1632-1675) was a Dutch painter. He liked to take simple scenes of indoor work or leisure, softly lit by daylight from a window, and paint them to perfection. His pictures are usually small (this one is only 24 centimetres high and 21 centimetres wide), and he did not paint very many.

Experiment with the Air Pump

Joseph Wright (1734-1797) was famous for his lighting effects. He worked out a system with screens so that he could sit in normal light himself to paint a candlelit scene. In this dramatic picture, a travelling scientist shows how air can be pumped out of the glass bowl, and let back just in time to save the breathless dove.

Norham Castle, Sunrise

Joseph Mallord William Turner (1775-1851) was fascinated by the effects of light and weather in the atmosphere. He often painted at Norham Castle, on the River Tweed between England and Scotland, and this oil sketch was made there towards the end of his life.

Paris, the Boulevard Montmartre at Night

Camille Pissarro (1830-1903) was a good friend of other impressionist painters such as Monet. He liked painting scenes looking along a road, but this is his only night-time picture. He painted it from a high window at the end of the street.

Nocturne in Blue and Gold, Old Battersea Bridge

James Whistler (1834-1903) was born in America. He painted a series of 'Nocturnes' to celebrate the beauty of the night. He said 'The evening mist clothes the riverside with poetry, like a veil; ... fairyland is before us.' His work had a mixed reception at first. The art critic Ruskin accused him of 'flinging a pot of paint in the public's face'.

Landscape with Human Figure

Mariano Fortuny (1838-1874) died young but was already recognised as the best painter of his time in Spain. As a young man, he spent a few years in Morocco and there he became familiar with the challenge of painting in very bright light.

The Beach at Trouville

Claude Monet (1840-1926) made this painting in July 1870 during a seaside holiday with his new wife Camille (on the left in the picture), and friends. Monet painted the picture on the beach: there are grains of sand still stuck in the paint.

The Dance

Paula Rego (born in 1935) grew up in Portugal, where this painting is set. It draws strongly on memories of childhood, growing up and marriage. The daughter, mother and grandmother in the background stand for the three ages of woman, and the whole painting represents the dance of life.

Index